The white dog and the black cat

The friendship - Volume I

Ladimir Luiz Marchioretto

Dedication

This book was dedicated to Billy, a little poodle who left us on January 7, 2020, after having kept us company for sixteen long and happy years.

Worthy of tributes much bigger than a childish story, the dog that was almost a person will be revered with other works soon.

The story tells of the real friendship that was born between him and the cat and some fictional passages. In addition to a second volume talking about the friendship, I will launch a book on the dog's full life.

Wherever you are, Billy, know that we still love you and that we miss you very much your beautiful face, your unique way, the affection that we may never feel coming from another animal.

Life goes on, albeit with much less brilliance. Who knows if we will not meet again, someday, somewhere?

Be happy.

Close to completing sixteen years old, the life of the little dog called Billy was always very good and happy.

If animals could express their emotions like humans, he would certainly smiling almost all the time.

Even though he was no longer a baby, the little poodle loved winning lap and staying close to his humans.

Always very wanted, he returned the care received and demonstrated all the love he felt in the heart.

When he was not eating ration or other snack, Billy loved sleeping hours and hours without any concern.

Having two beds, he could choose the most comfortable between the bedroom and the kitchen.

The white dog also loved walking in the patio of his house and looking at the street.

He was always very attentive to movement and knowing many animals walking through the neighborhood.

Several people liked Billy and talked with him while passing in front of the iron grid.

However, even as much loved by his owners, he needed some friends to toy with.

The Poodle would wag the tail to every people passing by and, sometimes, barked to call attention.

Billy had some friends but, like him, the most times not leave because of the iron grids that protected their houses.

They could only see each other when they walked with their humans, then they wagged their tails to demonstrate that they were friends.

One day, when he was distracted looking at nothing, a black cat approached and looked at the white dog.

The cat did not have friends because he had moved to that neighborhood a few days ago.

        The black cat enjoyed the white dog and began
waving the tail even without knowing if they could be
friends.

        He knew that not all dogs like cats, but that little
poodle seemed to be wanted and friendly.

Billy, which was same "good guy", liked animals without making any distinction.

As soon as he saw the cat on the other side of the iron grid, he approached and began to shake his small tail.

Both the white dog and the black cat were imagining how good it would be if they could toy together without that iron grid in the middle.

They could run, walk the square or even sleep one next to the other.

As he still needed to know the new neighborhood, the black cat left the front of the house of the white dog.

He wanted to know the goods things of the streets and, mainly, see what the best roofs to climb and sleep.

Being alone in the courtyard again, Billy decides to enter the home.

It was almost time to take one of his several daily naps, but before he needed to eat ration.

The next day, the white dog was to the lawn of his house again, but he could not see the black cat.

He could not imagine where his friend was, since there were many roofs and streets in the neighborhood.

However, while Billy was taking a long nap on one of his beds, the black cat passed in front of his house. He too missing his new friend, but do not could reviewing him.

The black cat, which has a collar with the name "Gum" recorded, walked around the streets and returned to Billy's house later.

He was very happy to see the dog, which had already awakened from another snooze.

As soon as Billy seen his happy friend, he approached the iron grid and both shake the tails.

It seemed that they were old friends, even if they had just been known for a few days.

As the tail cat's was bigger than the dog's, it made more wind when he moved it.

Again, they wished that there was not the iron grid, when they could toying on the square or on the streets of the neighborhood where they living.

Who knows if they could not meet on the street someday, then they could enjoy the new friendship?

One day, Billy and his human go walking the square, when the two friends finally were to be close to each other.

Happy, Gum followed the dog's steps as if he also belong to the man of whom he did not even know the name.

        At the end of afternoon, after the long and joyful walk, the white dog entered his house because he needed to rest.

        Alone on the sidewalk, the black cat climbed at the roof of a house in front of his friend's and waited much time, so he fell asleep.

The white dog and the black cat were anxiously to the next day.

Even not being of the same species, the strong friendship that was born will resist time and, as soon as they met on the street, they would have fun in the same way the children make.

The end

Published books in English

A train at dawn
A new star in the sky
Back to the beginning
Reflections in a moonlight night
The mansion of nightmares
The mystery of the mask
The sweet mystery of silence
The vampire kiss
The white dog and the black cat